ILLUSTRATED BOOK
OF
EXPERIMENTS

CONTENTS

SOME WORDS OF ADVICE

* Ask an adult to help you, especially when you are trying out experiments which need matches.

* Wear old clothes when you are doing the experiments. Or wear an apron or old shirt to cover your clothes.

* Experiments with water are best done outside or over a sink.

* Always strike matches away from your body.

* Make sure that a match has gone out before you throw it away.

* Lighted candles must be carefully secured in a holder so that they cannot topple over. Make sure that candles are not put near articles which burn easily.

* Wear oven gloves when you are handling hot objects, or anything which needs heating up.

* Be careful when you are using scissors, knives or any other pointed or cutting instruments.

* When you have finished the experiments, carefully put away the materials you have been using and wash your hands.

THE DIVER IN THE BOTTLE

Water, like other liquids, cannot be compressed. However, it is possible to compress air. Blowing up the tyres of a motor bike is an example of using compressed air.

To make your diver, you need:
a glass jar with a wide neck
a transparent plastic tube with a top
aluminium foil
an elastic band, a balloon
a hammer and a nail
scissors, glue, a felt-tip pen

Completely fill the jar with water.

Use the hammer and nail to make a small hole in the top of the plastic tube.

Using the felt-tip pen, draw a small figure on a sheet of aluminium foil.
Make sure that the figure is not larger than the tube.
Cut it out and glue it on to the outside of the tube. Now you have your diver.

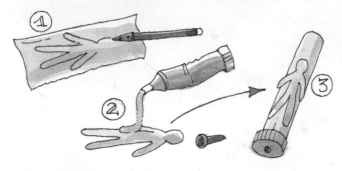

Fill the tube with enough water so that when it is turned upside down, it floats in the jar.

Cut a piece of balloon.
Fix it tightly over the neck of the jar with the elastic band.

Press the palm of your hand onto the covered opening of the jar... and watch what happens now.
The diver starts to dive. When you remove your hand, he comes back to the surface.
Do you know why this happens? Watch the space in the tube which does not contain water. What happens when you push on the neck of the jar?
This space fills with water. The tube becomes heavier and so it sinks.

A submarine has enormous tanks. When they contain air, it floats. When they are filled with water, it dives.

A HOT AIR BALLOON

Hot air is lighter than cold air. That is why hot air rises. You can see this happen if you hold a toy windmill above a candle flame. The sails of the windmill slowly start to turn.

To make your balloon, you need:
two identical paper bags
a hair dryer
a piece of string
a small, straight stick
sticky tape

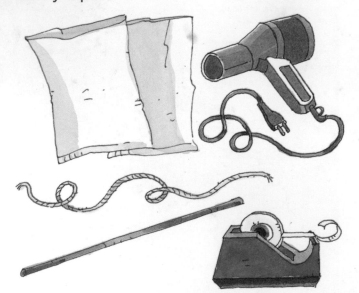

Use the stick and the string to make a balance.
Do this by tying the string in the middle of the stick.

The balance will always go down on the side with the heaviest object on it.

Use the sticky tape to fix a paper bag upside down on each end of the stick. The open end of the bags should be at the bottom. The two bags are identical, so their weight is identical. The stick is therefore balanced.

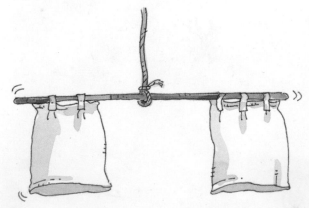

Hang your balance from some object high up. This leaves your hands free. You could hold it in one hand, but this makes it more difficult to do the experiment.
Make sure that the two bags are still balanced. (They should be at the same level.)

You can decorate the paper bag and paint your initials on it. Take it off the balance and fill it with hot air from the hair dryer.
Let it go and – who knows? Perhaps it will cross the sea!

Plug in the hair dryer. Now blow the hot air into the opening of one paper bag. You will see that the bag rises immediately.
Can you explain this?

Hot air balloons often have bright colours. Under the balloon there is a basket for the passengers. Before it will lift into the sky, the balloon must be filled with hot air.

A GLASS ORGAN

Sound is made up of tiny vibrations. When you pluck the strings of a guitar, they start to vibrate. The vibrations of the strings make the surrounding air vibrate. You cannot see these vibrations but you can hear them.

To make this glass organ, you need:
eight wine glasses
a jug filled with water

Half fill a wine glass with water.
Wash your hands and dry them well.
Moisten your index finger.
Now slowly slide your finger round the rim of the glass.
Carry on doing this until you hear a continuous sound.

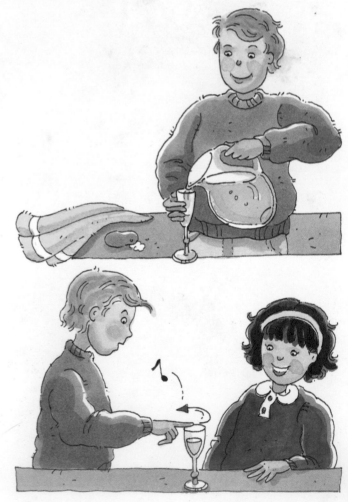

You get a ringing sound when your finger rubs against protruding bits on the rim. This makes the glass start to vibrate.

Now pour some water into another glass. Make sure that the second glass contains more water than the first.
Now you know how to make a glass 'sing', do this with the second glass. Do you get the same sound as you did from the half-filled glass?
No, the sound is higher.
The tone of the sound therefore depends on the level of water in the glass. The more water, the higher the sound.

Now put the eight glasses side by side. Pour in different levels of water so that you get a scale.
Here are the notes of a scale:
do-re-mi-fa-so-la-ti-do.

Be very precise. The organ must not play wrong notes. You have to tune the organ by adding or taking away some water, until you have got the tone you want. Then you can try to play a well-known tune on it.

All musical instruments produce sound vibrations when they are played.

The double bass produces deeper notes than its cousin, the violin.

A SUPERSONIC PLANE

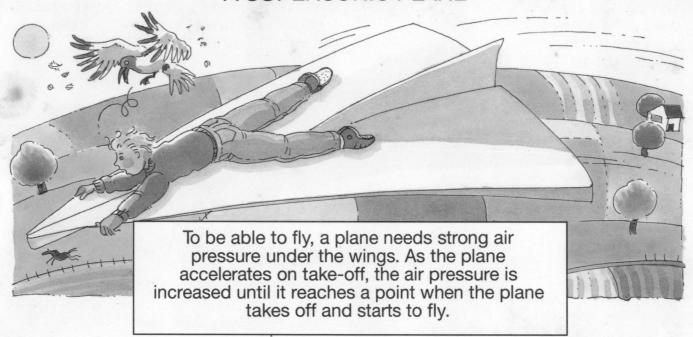

To be able to fly, a plane needs strong air pressure under the wings. As the plane accelerates on take-off, the air pressure is increased until it reaches a point when the plane takes off and starts to fly.

To make your plane, you need:
a sheet of paper (20 × 25 cm)
sticky tape
a pencil and a ruler

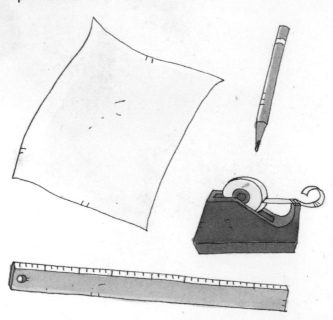

Put down the sheet with the fold on the right. Find the middle of each short side and link them with a line.
Now draw two lines from the beginning of this line, at the fold, to the middle of each long edge. Fold along these. (diagram 2)

Fold over the short edge of the paper three times. This gives you a rigid edge. It will be the nose of the plane. (diagram 1)

Fold back either side along the first line you drew. (diagram 3)

Draw a dotted line like the one shown on diagram 4.
Fold the paper inwards along the dotted line.
This will be the tail of your plane.
(diagram 4)

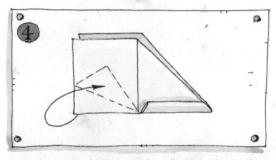

Look carefully at the following drawing. Draw the folding line shown on each side. Fold the paper outwards along these lines to make the wings. (diagram 5)

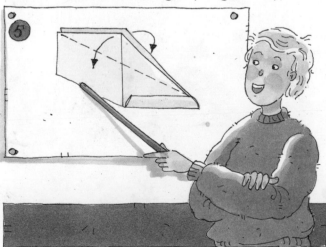

Now draw the last folding line, fold out the wings along it, make the back part of the plane stand up and – fasten your seat belts! (diagram 6)

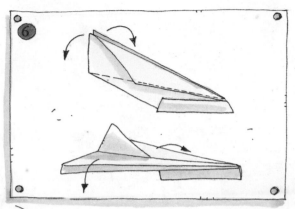

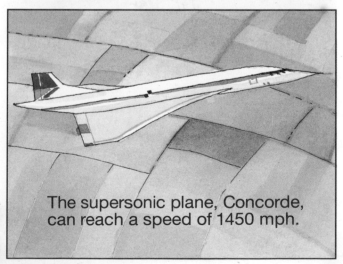

The supersonic plane, Concorde, can reach a speed of 1450 mph.

THE MAGICAL EFFECTS OF WATER

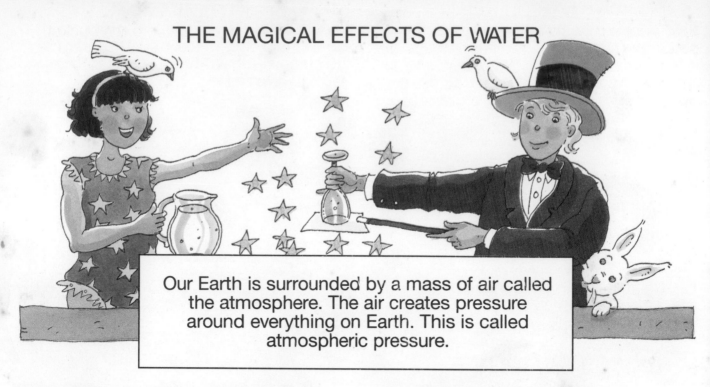

Our Earth is surrounded by a mass of air called the atmosphere. The air creates pressure around everything on Earth. This is called atmospheric pressure.

To do these experiments, you need:
a glass
a jug of water
a piece of paper
a bucket
a chewed piece of chewing gum

First experiment
Fill the glass to the brim with water. Cover the glass with the piece of paper and put your hand over it.

Slowly turn the glass upside down in a single movement, holding the paper against the rim with the palm of your hand.

Take away your hand and – if you have done the trick properly, the water will stay in the glass. Can you explain this? The air creates pressure on the paper, so that the water cannot escape from the glass. In case it goes wrong, it would be best to try this trick over a bucket.

Second experiment
Pour water into the bucket until it is just over half full.

Crumple a piece of paper. Stick it with chewing gum inside the bottom of the glass; turn the glass upside down.

Carefully lower the glass into the bucket.

Remove the glass. The paper has stayed dry. This is because the glass is full of air. This air causes pressure and prevents the water from getting in. Therefore the paper stays dry.

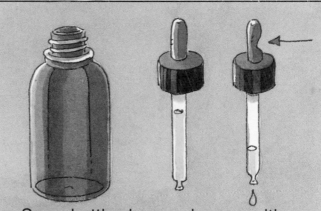

Some bottles have a dropper with a rubber bulb. To fill the dropper with liquid, it is held in the bottle and the bulb is squeezed. The dropper fills with liquid and the air pressure keeps it in. The bulb is pressed again to empty it of liquid.

WHEN WATER RISES

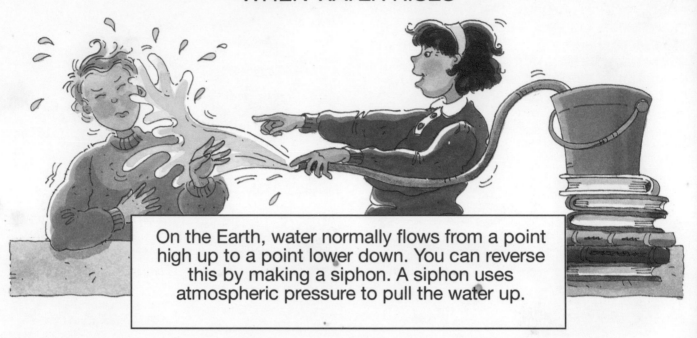

On the Earth, water normally flows from a point high up to a point lower down. You can reverse this by making a siphon. A siphon uses atmospheric pressure to pull the water up.

To make a siphon, you need:
one metre of rubber tube
two big glass jars
some large books

Pile up the books.

Pour water into one jar until it is half full. Put the jar on the books.

Put the empty jar in front of the books. This jar must be lower down than the jar with water in it. That is very important for the experiment.

Completely fill the rubber tube with water. Make sure that there are no bubbles in the tube. Block the ends of the tube by putting your thumbs over them.

Plunge the two ends into the two jars. Let go of both ends at the same time. Now the water flows from one bottle to the other.
You have made a water siphon. What happens to the water?

Watch the water carefully. The water in the jar on the books rises up the tube until it gets to the highest point. From there it flows down on its own.

If a car runs out of petrol, it is possible to use this method to siphon petrol from the tank of another car.

THE EXPANSION OF A COIN

Many things become a bit bigger when they are heated up. This is called 'expansion'. When things expand, they obviously take up more room. When they cool down, they shrink again.

To do this experiment, you need:
a coin
a paper clip
a candle, some matches
two small pieces of wood
a hammer, five or six nails
some wire
a felt-tip pen
oven gloves

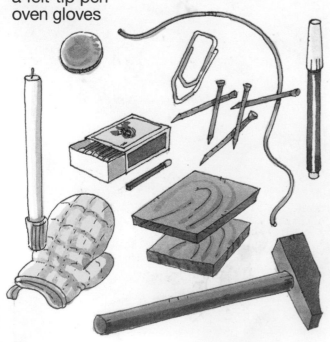

Put the coin in the middle of a piece of wood. With the pen, make a mark on the wood at either side of the coin.

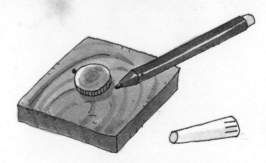

Remove the coin and hammer a nail into each of the two pen marks.

Nail the other piece of wood onto it.

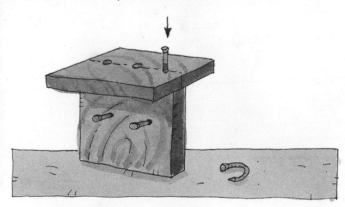

Now attach the wire to the paper clip and slide the coin into the paper clip.

Light the candle. Pick up the wire with the coin on it. Hold the coin in the flame for one minute. Don't forget to wear the oven glove.

Don't touch the coin with your fingers. It will be far too hot. You could burn yourself.

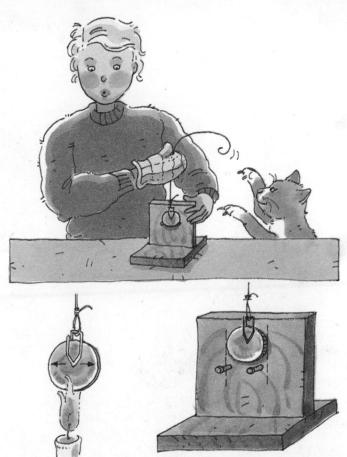

Now try to slide the coin between the two nails. It is impossible. You can see that the coin has expanded.

There are spaces between the lengths of rail on a railway line. The rails will expand in hot weather.

A SHOWER OF MARBLES

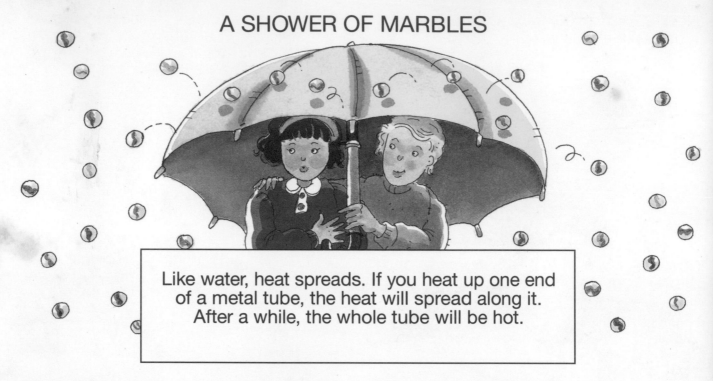

Like water, heat spreads. If you heat up one end of a metal tube, the heat will spread along it. After a while, the whole tube will be hot.

You need:
a thin metal tube 50 cm long (or a curtain rod)
4 marbles
a candle, some matches
oven gloves

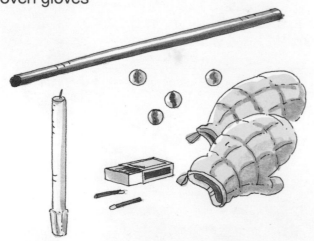

Take the metal tube and fix one of the marbles 5 cm from the end, using a little candle wax.

To stick the marbles on with wax, just take a small piece of wax and squash it between your fingers. After a little while the wax softens so that you can mould it.

It is then easy to stick the marbles to the metal tube with the wax.

Next, stick the other marbles along the tube, 3 cm from each other.

This happens because the heat travels along the tube. The heat melts the wax on the first marble, then the second, and so on...

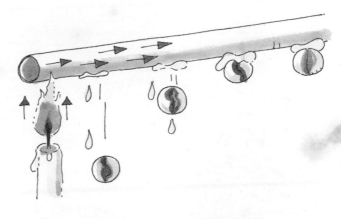

Light the candle. Put on oven gloves.

You now know why you need to wear oven gloves!

Put the end of the tube in the flame. Now look what happens. The marbles fall off one by one.

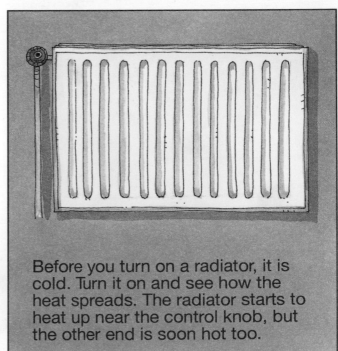

Before you turn on a radiator, it is cold. Turn it on and see how the heat spreads. The radiator starts to heat up near the control knob, but the other end is soon hot too.

A PERISCOPE

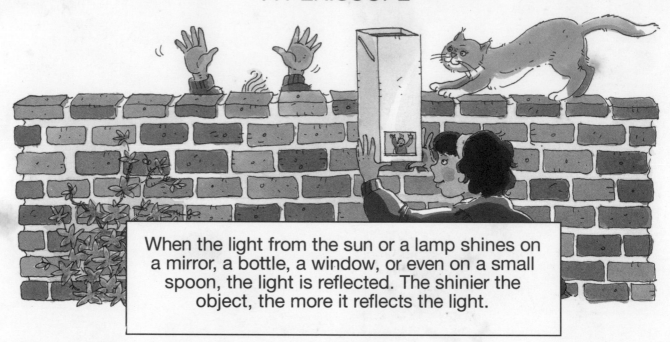

When the light from the sun or a lamp shines on a mirror, a bottle, a window, or even on a small spoon, the light is reflected. The shinier the object, the more it reflects the light.

To make your periscope, you need:
two small square mirrors
a sheet of cardboard (30 × 30 cm)
some sticky tape
a felt-tip pen
a ruler

Draw a line down the middle of the cardboard so that you divide it in two. Then draw a line on each side to divide each half into two equal parts. The sheet is now divided into quarters.

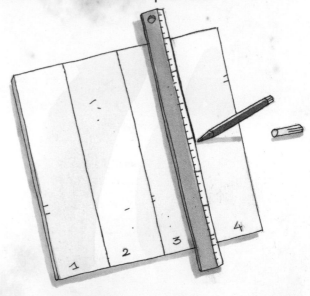

Draw a square measuring 7 × 7 cm at the top of the second quarter on the sheet and at the bottom of the fourth quarter, as shown on the following page.

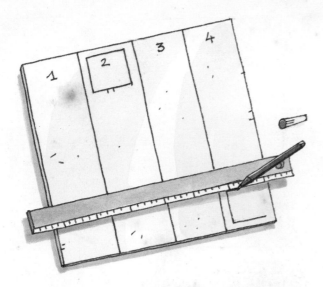

Now slide the mirrors into the slots and fix them with sticky tape. Make sure that the reflective sides of the mirrors are turned towards the inside of the periscope.

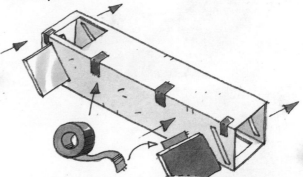

In the first and third quarters, draw four slots like letter boxes. Again, look carefully at the illustration. The width of the slots must not be greater than the width of the mirrors. They should make an angle of 45° with the side of the cardboard. You may have to ask someone to help you with this.

Now cut out the two squares and the four slots.

Your periscope is ready. If you hold it upright, you can look over a wall or your Mum's head. If you hold it on its side, you can look round corners without being seen.

Fold the cardboard along the lines to form a rectangular box. Stick the box together with sticky tape.

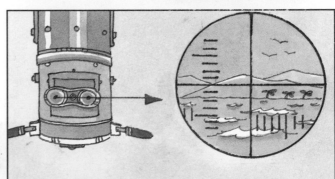

The crew of a submarine uses a periscope to see above them on the surface of the water.

A SIMPLE CAMERA

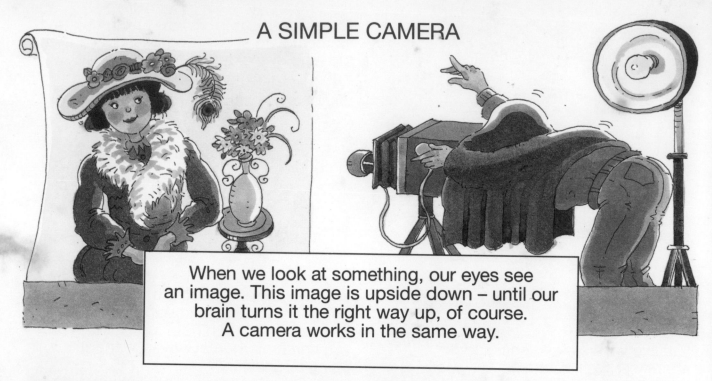

When we look at something, our eyes see an image. This image is upside down – until our brain turns it the right way up, of course. A camera works in the same way.

To make your camera, you need:
a small shoebox
a felt-tip pen
a nail, sticky tape
some tracing paper
a small magnifying glass (not essential)
a large black cloth

With the nail, make a hole in the bottom of the shoebox.
Make sure that the hole is right in the middle of the box.
If you have a magnifying glass, stick it over the hole, on the inside of the shoebox.

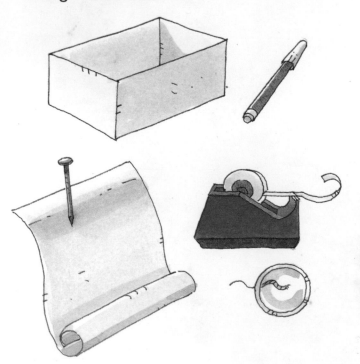

Put the tracing paper over the top of the box. Fix it on carefully with sticky tape.

You have made a simple camera. This type of camera is known by its Latin name, *camera obscura*. It was invented centuries ago. People used it to make drawings.

The hole in the box must be surrounded by darkness to get a photographic image. Use the black cloth to cover yourself and the box. Look towards the light from the tracing paper side.

Find an object which you want to 'photograph'. Hide yourself and your camera under the black cloth. Using a felt-tip pen with a flexible point, draw round the image which appears on the paper. Make sure that you do not press too hard, or you will pierce the paper. You will see that the drawing you have made is upside down.

The *camera obscura* is the fore-runner of modern cameras. It was discovered only 150 years ago that an image could be fixed on paper. This was the start of photography.

25

A FLOATING COMPASS

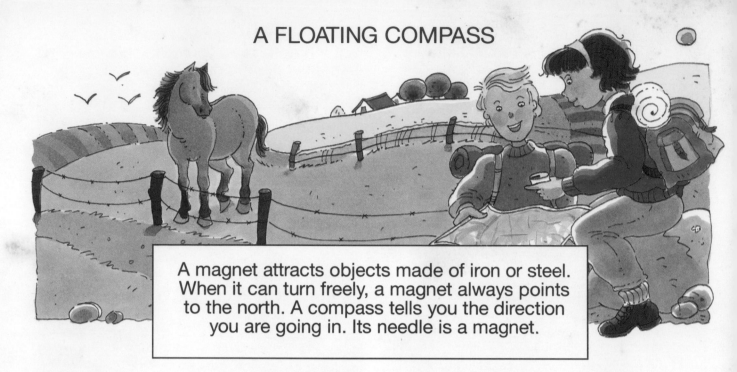

A magnet attracts objects made of iron or steel. When it can turn freely, a magnet always points to the north. A compass tells you the direction you are going in. Its needle is a magnet.

To make a compass, you need:
a small magnetic bar (magnetised)
a reel of cotton
a cork
a needle
a soup bowl
a kitchen knife

Tie the cotton in the middle of the magnetic bar. When you hold up the cotton, the magnetic bar should stay perfectly level.

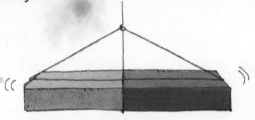

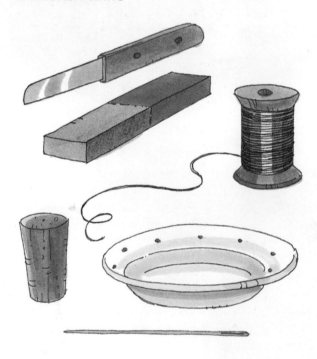

Turn the bar several times and then let it return to its original position.
You will notice that the ends (the poles) always point in the same direction.
One pole shows north and the other shows south.
You have made a simple compass. This is how the needle of a compass works.

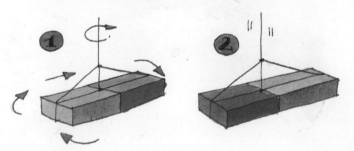

A magnet attracts many metal objects. Try for yourself. Would a needle act as a magnet?

Yes, but first you have to magnetise the needle. You can magnetise the needle by rubbing it about fifty times against the end of the magnet. It must always be rubbed in the same direction. Draw the magnet along the needle, take it round in a curve at some distance from the needle, and put it back on the needle.

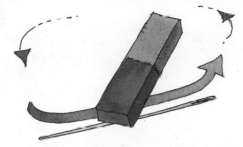

You can now see that a needle can be magnetised effectively. Will it attract another needle?

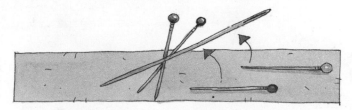

If it does you can now make your floating compass.

Cut a slice off the cork.

Stick the needle through it. Fill the soup bowl with water. Put the slice of cork into the middle of the bowl and let it turn freely. The needle always points in the same direction: one way is north, the other is south.

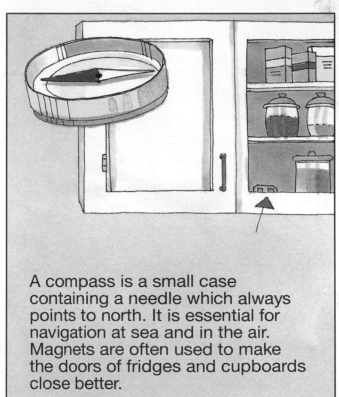

A compass is a small case containing a needle which always points to north. It is essential for navigation at sea and in the air. Magnets are often used to make the doors of fridges and cupboards close better.

THE ELECTRIC COMB

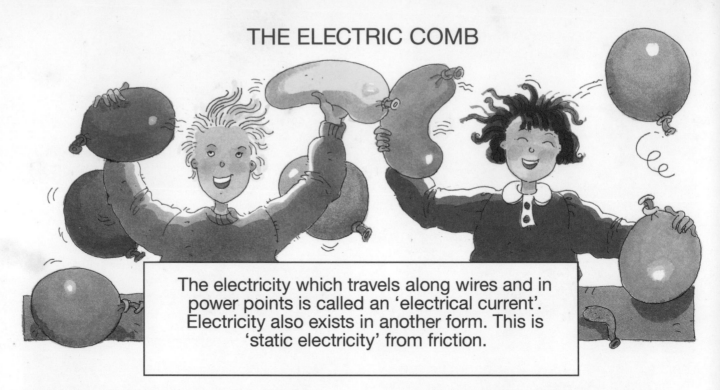

The electricity which travels along wires and in power points is called an 'electrical current'. Electricity also exists in another form. This is 'static electricity' from friction.

To produce static electricity, you need:
a comb
some small scraps of paper
a balloon
a woollen sweater

Comb your hair for at least a minute. Then put your comb over your head. Your hair stands up on end. The friction of the comb has an electric charge. It is this electricity which attracts your hair towards the comb.

Put the scraps of paper onto the table. Put on the sweater and scrape the comb against the wool.

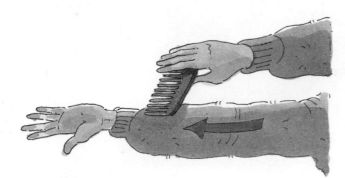

Now put the 'electric' comb over the paper scraps. They are attracted by the comb and stick to it.

Blow up a balloon and tie a knot in it. You can make it into an 'electric' balloon by rubbing it against the sweater. It will then attract the paper scraps, fix itself to a wall, or do something even more spectacular.

Turn on the tap on the washbasin so that you get a thin stream of water. Hold the balloon close to the water. You will see that the water is attracted to it.

When you take off your jumper, you will hear crackling sounds. This is also caused by static electricity. It is quite harmless.

Factory chimneys are very high so the smoke which comes out does not blow against the walls of buildings nearby. This would result in static electricity and particles of smoke would stick to the walls.

INVISIBLE INK

Metal which is left outside soon goes rusty. When we burn wood, it turns to ashes. Changes of this sort are called chemical changes.

To make 'invisible' ink, you need:
a lemon squeezer and a lemon
a desk lamp
two sheets of white paper
a pen and nib
a fine paintbrush
a bowl

Squeeze out the lemon juice. Pour it into the bowl.

Dip the paintbrush in the lemon juice and paint your name on one sheet of paper. Your writing is obviously more difficult to read than if you had written in blue ink.

When the lemon juice has dried, there is nothing to see on the paper. Has your name disappeared? Not at all. It has simply become invisible. But you can make it reappear as if by magic.

Switch on the desk lamp.
Hold the paper in front of the lamp for several minutes. The heat of the bulb makes your name reappear.

By a chemical process, the lemon juice goes brown more quickly than the paper.

Invisible ink allows you to send secret messages to your friends or your parents. It could also be used to draw a map for finding hidden treasure! It is a fascinating thought.

Messages are written with a pen. Drawings are painted with a paintbrush. Don't forget to show your friends how they can make the invisible ink visible. Tell them to be patient as well. It takes a little while before the heat of the lamp makes the message written in lemon juice appear.

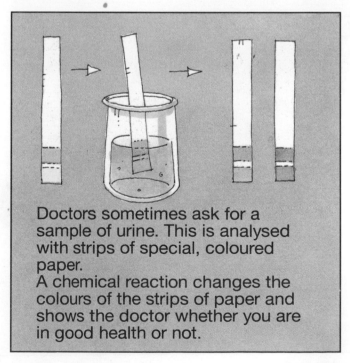

Doctors sometimes ask for a sample of urine. This is analysed with strips of special, coloured paper.
A chemical reaction changes the colours of the strips of paper and shows the doctor whether you are in good health or not.

31

HIDDEN COLOURS

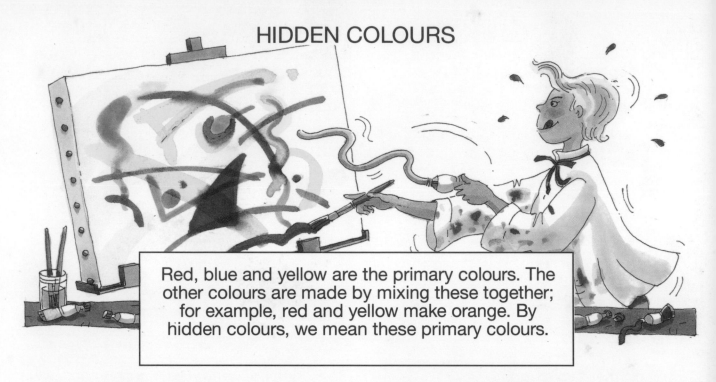

Red, blue and yellow are the primary colours. The other colours are made by mixing these together; for example, red and yellow make orange. By hidden colours, we mean these primary colours.

To find the hidden colours, you need:
a plastic container for water
coloured felt-tip pens
some large paper coffee filters
scissors
two bottles
clothes pegs
a piece of string

You are going to find the hidden colours which make up the colours of your pens. Fill the container with water. Put one bottle on each side of the container. Stretch the string between the bottles and tie each end round a bottle neck.

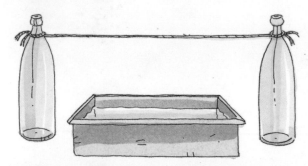

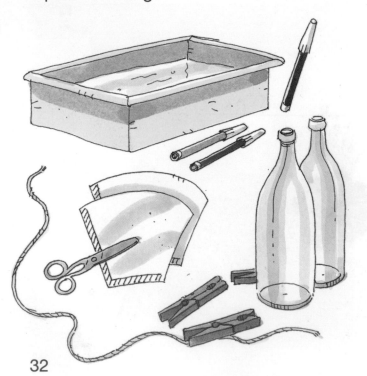

Open the coffee filters and cut strips of 30 × 4 cm. You need a strip for each colour that you want to analyse.

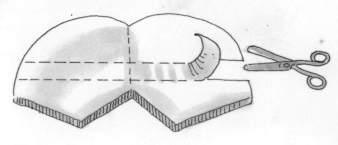

Draw a dot in the colour you want to analyse 4 cm from the bottom of each strip.

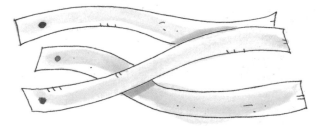

Attach the strips to the string with clothes pegs. Make sure that the dots you have drawn are just above the surface of the water.

As the water is absorbed several streaks of different colours appear on the strips. These are the hidden colours which make up the colours you are analysing.

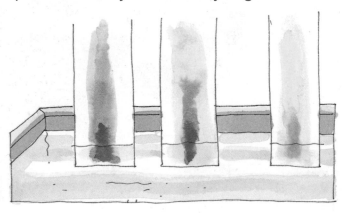

When the streaks of colour reach the top of the strips, you can remove them and leave them to dry. Later, you can compare the different strips.

The hidden colours spread when the filter papers absorb water from the container. The water soaks into the coloured dots and sends the colours towards the edges of the strips. Some colours have several hidden colours because they have to be mixed again and again to get the shade.

Do you know which colour is made up of all three hidden colours? (Black!)

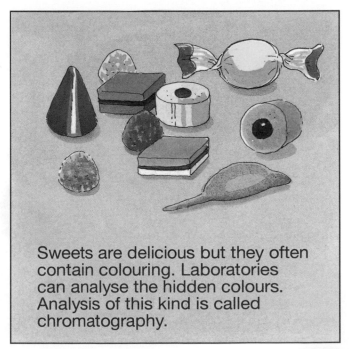

Sweets are delicious but they often contain colouring. Laboratories can analyse the hidden colours. Analysis of this kind is called chromatography.

33

SHADOW PUPPETS

Water and glass allow sunlight or the light from a lamp to pass through. They are transparent. Objects made of wood, metal or cardboard, for example, do not let light through. They are opaque and shadows form behind them.

To make shadow puppets, you need:
some cardboard
scissors
some thin sticks
sticky tape
a spotlight
an old white sheet
a felt-tip pen

The best shadow puppet effects are made in a dark room. Hang the white sheet in such a way that you can get behind it. You need to be between the spotlight and the sheet. Try different positions to find out how far away you should be. If you want big shadows, you need to be further away from the sheet.

You can make superb shadows just by using your hands. Try to copy the shadows in the picture. Your hands have to be in exactly the same position to get the best effect.

It is quite simple to make effective puppets for a show. On a piece of cardboard draw the outline of a cowboy, a clown, a plane, or whatever you want. Cut out the figures and attach them to the sticks with sticky tape.

You could also cut out a cardboard hat. Put the hat on one hand, a short distance from the sheet and make gestures with the other hand.
You could also make a magician with a magic wand.

To show a cook, cut the shape of a chef's hat out of cardboard. You can also cut out a wooden spoon.

Write a short story which includes all your characters.
Invite your friends and sit them on the other side of the sheet. They will see silhouettes of the puppets.

You could use a white sheet to reflect light and prevent shadows falling onto the objects when taking a photograph.

A CANDLE COMPETITION

A fire cannot burn without air. You may have seen people using bellows to blow air on to an open fire or a barbecue. This makes the fire burn better.

For the candle competition, you need:
three candles of exactly the same length,
two jars, one big and one small (with their lids)
one small lid, matches
plasticine

Put the candles on the three lids. Fix them in place with the plasticine.

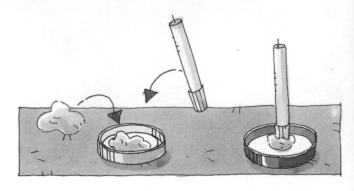

Put the candles and lids in a safe place, where nothing can catch fire – on an empty draining board near the kitchen sink, for example.

Fire can be very dangerous, so be very careful. An adult should be with you when you do this experiment.

36

Strike a match and light the three candles.
Leave one candle uncovered.
Put the two jars over the other candles.
Make sure that the jars have the right lids.

Which of the candles burns for the longest time?

The uncovered candle wins the competition. It carries on burning until it

has completely melted away. There is enough air around it to keep the flame burning. The candles under the jars go out more quickly, but the candle under the big jar has more air around it so it burns for longer than the candle under the small jar.

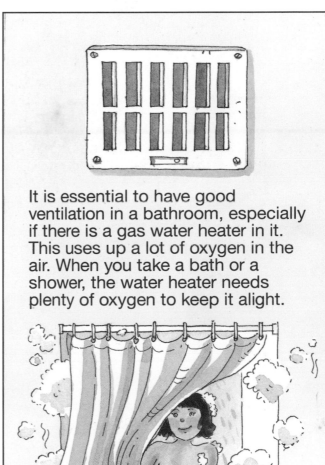

It is essential to have good ventilation in a bathroom, especially if there is a gas water heater in it. This uses up a lot of oxygen in the air. When you take a bath or a shower, the water heater needs plenty of oxygen to keep it alight.

A MAZE

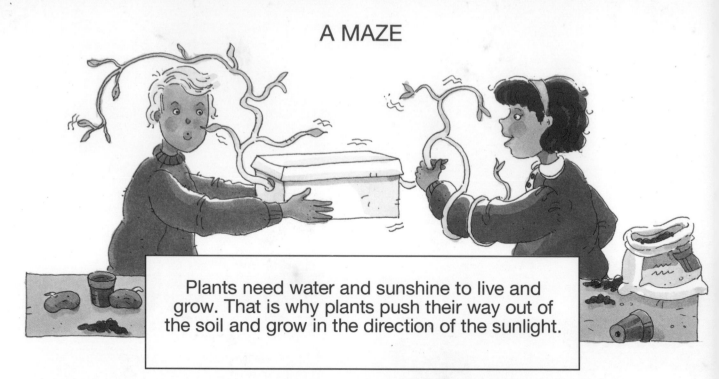

Plants need water and sunshine to live and grow. That is why plants push their way out of the soil and grow in the direction of the sunlight.

To make a potato maze, you need:
one potato
some compost
a shoebox
a small flowerpot
some cardboard
scissors
sticky tape

If you can find a potato which is sprouting, you can start immediately. If not, put the potato in a damp place. After a few days, you will notice that the potato has produced some whitish-purple stalks. These are the shoots.

Cut three small cardboard rectangles which exactly match the width of the box. In each rectangle, cut a small door. Fix each rectangle to the inside of the box.

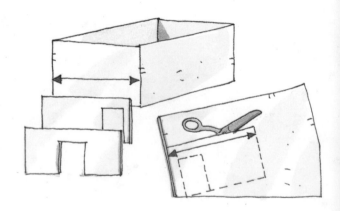

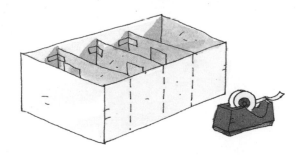

Make a small hole at one end of the shoebox.

Put a little compost in the flowerpot and plant the potato in it, leaving the longest shoot sticking out of the earth. Be careful not to damage the shoot.

Put the pot inside the box, at the end that does not have the hole.

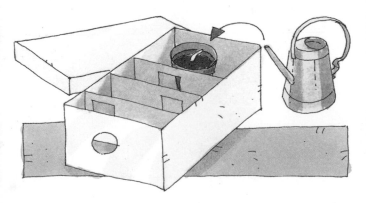

Then close the box and put it in a sunny place.

Be patient, and after a few days you will see that the shoot has found its way to the outside.
Now remove the lid of the box. The potato has forced its way through the maze.
During the days of darkness, it grew in the direction of the light.

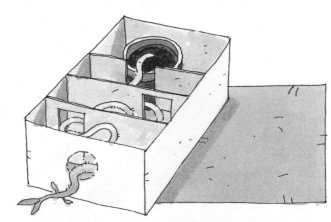

Many types of vegetable grow best in a greenhouse, where it is hot, damp and full of light.

THE PARACHUTE TEST

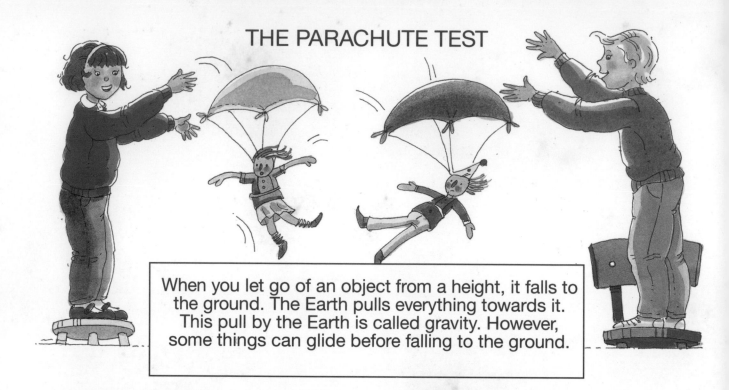

When you let go of an object from a height, it falls to the ground. The Earth pulls everything towards it. This pull by the Earth is called gravity. However, some things can glide before falling to the ground.

To carry out a parachute test, you need:
some sheets of paper
sticky tape
a reel of cotton
a matchbox
plasticine
scissors

You are going to make three sorts of parachute and then find out which one glides for the longest time.

First choose a high place which you can let the parachutes fall from; standing half-way up the stairs, for example.
For the test to be effective, all three parachutes must be dropped from the same height.

You are going to hang a weighted matchbox from each of the parachutes you make. Which of these parachutes will stay in the air the longest?

40

First parachute

Weigh down the matchboxes with a small piece of plasticine. Make sure that you use the same amount for all three parachutes.

Take a sheet of paper measuring 20 × 20 cm and crumple it. Use sticky tape to fix lengths of cotton of 25 cm each to the four corners. Attach the other ends of the cotton to the matchbox. Drop your parachute and don't forget to count the time it takes to reach the ground.

Second parachute

Take an uncrumpled sheet of paper measuring 20 × 20 cm. Use the sticky tape to fix the 25 cm lengths of cotton to the four corners. Attach the other ends of the cotton to the matchbox.
Drop the parachute and count…

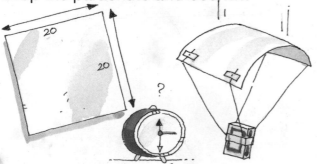

Third parachute

Take a sheet of paper measuring 30 × 20 cm. Make a parachute with the four 25 cm lengths of cotton and the matchbox, as you did before.

The biggest parachute is the one which stays in the air for longest. The air under the sheet keeps it up. Instead of falling, it glides slowly down towards the ground.

Air passing under the big wings of a hang-glider keeps the pilot in flight. He glides slowly down towards the ground.

THE FLOATING NEEDLE

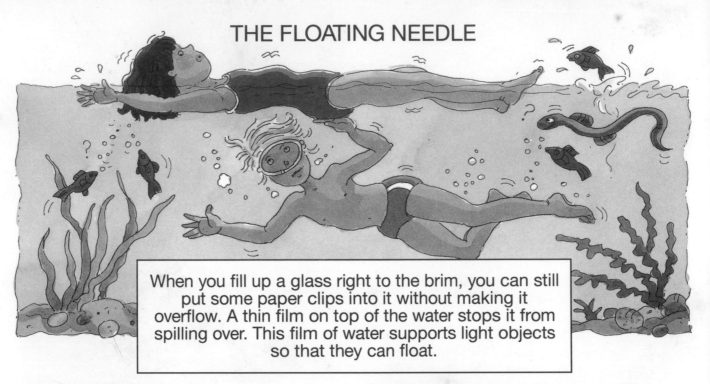

When you fill up a glass right to the brim, you can still put some paper clips into it without making it overflow. A thin film on top of the water stops it from spilling over. This film of water supports light objects so that they can float.

To do this experiment, you need:
a clean container
a needle
a fork
a jug of water
a glass
several paper clips
a cotton handkerchief
an elastic band

Fill the glass to the brim with water. Slowly drop the paper clips in one by one. It takes a while to do this so that the water does not overflow.
Can you see how the surface of the water begins to rise slightly above the rim of the glass?

Now try the floating needle experiment.
Fill the container with water.

Lay the needle across the prongs of the fork.

Gently lower the prongs of the fork into the water. If you do this carefully enough, the needle will float on the surface of the water.

Why does this happen?
The fork breaks the film on the water, but it re-forms under the needle. The film is strong enough to support the weight of the needle. If you look closely, you will notice that the film is slightly dented by the needle, but it does not break.

You can try another experiment to test the film of water theory.
Fill a glass almost to the top with water.

Stretch the handkerchief over the glass and fix it on with the elastic band.

Turn the glass upside down and – the water stays in the glass!

Water-skaters can run across the surface of water on a pond without sinking. The film on the water is strong enough to support their weight.

WHERE DOES THE WIND COME FROM?

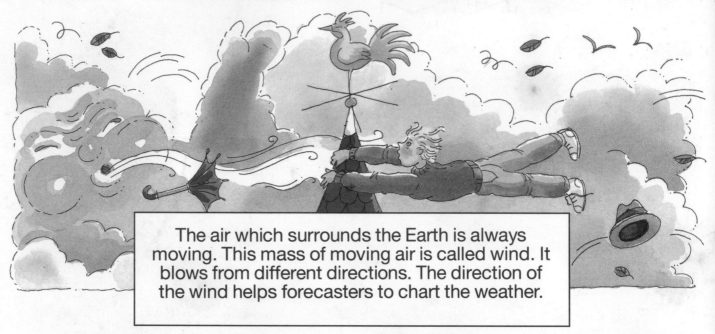

The air which surrounds the Earth is always moving. This mass of moving air is called wind. It blows from different directions. The direction of the wind helps forecasters to chart the weather.

To make a weathervane, you need:
a pencil with a small rubber on the end
plasticine, a pin
a large yoghurt pot
a block of wood (30 × 30 cm)
scissors and sticky tape
a thin sheet of cardboard
a drinking straw
a compass

Stick a little plasticine onto the middle of a block of wood.

Pierce the base of the yoghurt pot with the pencil and push the point of the pencil into the plasticine on the wood. Stick some plasticine round the rim of the yoghurt pot. This will make the whole thing steadier.

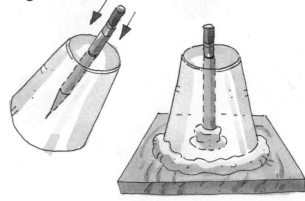

Make a cut at each end of the straw. Cut out two triangles from the cardboard. Put one triangle in each cut. Fix them firmly in place with sticky tape.

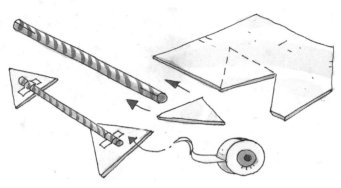

Stick the pin through the middle of the straw and into the rubber on the end of the pencil.

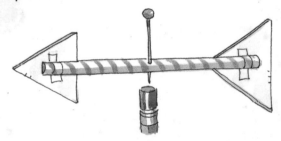

Position the weathervane outside your house with the compass next to it. On the wooden block, mark north with N, south with S, west with W, and east with E.

Weather forecasters always describe the wind by the direction it is coming from. This means that a north wind blows towards the south, and a west wind blows to the east.

Each day, note the wind direction on a piece of paper. You can then see if there is a connection between the wind direction and the weather.

The cockerel weathervane on some churches shows the wind direction.

This photograph was taken by a meteorological satellite which gravitates around the Earth taking photos of the winds.

Original edition:
© MCMXC by Zuidnederlandse Uitgeverij N.V.,
Aartselaar, Belgium. All rights reserved.
This edition:
© MCMXC by Invader Ltd., Chichester PO20 7EQ,
England. All rights reserved.